First Days and Failures

Jessica Anders
Illustrated by Tim Hodge

stonetowerpress.com

First Days and Failures

Stone Tower Press
7 Ellen Rd.
Middletown, RI 02842
stonetowerpress.com

Paperback ISBN: 978-1-7368651-2-5

Formatting and cover design by Amy Cole, JPL Design Solutions

Cover and interior illustrations by Tim Hodge

Printed in the United States of America

Second printing

Dedicated to:

My parents for teaching me to laugh, to all of the amazing teachers I have had through the years (i.e., Mrs. Wilson and Ms. Longfellow) that gave me a smile on a bad day, and to my sweet students. Hang in there guys—it only gets better.

Table of Contents

Preface 7

School

1. Kindergarten: "What are they doing with their fingers?!" 9
2. "To Battle!"—Snakes vs. Pitchfork, Frisbee, and Rocks 11
3. New School, New Look 15
4. Doesn't Look Like It Tastes 17
5. The Cat Goes for a Ride 21
6. Using My Head 25
7. Almost Buried Alive 29
8. Rejection: Cute Boys and Seating Assignments 33
9. Middle School: The Nemesis of Rain Puddles 37
10. High School: Directionally and Vertically Challenged 41
11. Shaky Sets 45
12. Crosswalks and Close Calls 49

Summer Jobs

13. Summer Nanny: Dead Bunnies and the Discovery Channel 53

14. Pooping Directions 57
15. Prayer Requests: Santa vs. Jesus 61

Internships

16. The RA Adventures 65
17. As the Intern: Tornados, Lock-in Disasters, and Chasing a Tortoise 69
18. Handling the Snake: Why King Tut got Angry 73
19. Hunt, Cook, Eat: A Stream, a Rock and a Squirrel 77
20. Fish Funerals 81

Conclusion: It's Going to be OK 83
About the Author 85
About the Illustrator 85

Preface

This book is written in order to make you laugh and realize everyone messes up, things rarely go the way you think they should, and to not take it all too seriously.

Having worked with preteens and teenagers for somewhere near ten years now, I know that it can be easy for them to get tunnel vision. It's easy to get so caught up and focused on their own screw ups or embarrassments of the day that it feels like the world is ending. So I began telling my preteen Sunday School class my first day of school stories each August as school began. I wanted to let them see me laugh at myself and know that it all will be OK. If it was helpful to them, maybe it will be to you as well—or at least make you smile.

Aa Bb Cc Dd Ee Ff Gg H

1

Kindergarten: "What are they doing with their fingers?!"

I don't remember being anxious before we walked through the door. I was excited to read new books and play on the shiny playground we had passed on our way into the school.

My daddy held my hand as we walked in nice and slow with a big smile. We put my backpack on a hanger and my lunch in a cubby with my mat.

Startled, I looked around and saw that a boy had a finger in his nose. I wasn't sure why he would do this, but it bothered me. I stared at him for a minute, and tightened the grip upon my father's hand as I realized in horror that it was six or seven kids that were all suffering from this same insanity. Fingers were in noses everywhere I turned!

My father could sense my panic and got down on his knees at my level to ask what was wrong. I took a breath and said, "Daddy, I do not belong here!"

By the end of the year, my classmates had mastered the art of the Kleenex, and I had received my first lesson in the importance of hand sanitizer.

2

"To Battle!"—Snakes vs. Pitchfork, Frisbee, and Rocks

Clear cool water, clear blue sky, and a strong rope swing—it was the makings of a perfect day at the river. Our family and some friends were spending a few days at a cabin on the Sabinal River near Utopia, Texas. This was a time to get away and have fun in nature.

A short hike from the cabin, a rope swing dangled invitingly from a huge Lost Maple tree leaning over the river. The dads came down with us to this epicenter of fun. They watched from out in the waist-deep, slow-moving, clear river as we swung to them.

My turn to swing came. I was nervous, but mostly excited. All the others were boys, so there was no way I would show any fear. I grabbed the rope and hung on—and kept holding. I didn't let go a bit early as some kids had done. I didn't release it in the prime spot where it was deepest. I didn't let go even after the momentum shifted and swung me back toward the tree. My father called for me to brace myself as I headed into the trunk of the tree.

Incredibly, my legs came around and I pushed off with my feet and managed to shimmy down the rope with only a few abrasions.

As I dropped into the shallow water near the massive tree, everyone sighed with relief. But as I began wading back to the bank to get in line again, the real screaming began.

"Watch out!" "Don't step there!" "Stop moving! Now!"

Confused and frustrated, I tried to shuffle further out of the swing path, thinking that everyone was afraid I would get hit by the next person on the rope. I was wrong.

Suddenly, I saw the thrash of water next to me and heard a boy on shore scream, "Snake!!!!"

Snake was an understatement. This was the mammoth mother of all snakes.

Letting go of any pretense of bravery I had, I leapt from the water and ran behind the line of boys. Our dads scrambled out and pushed us further back, explaining that this was a water moccasin—a poisonous snake that could easily kill us if we had been bitten.

After a quick discussion among the dads, it was decided that the reptile could not be allowed to live. Its fate was sealed. But how best to dispatch it using the limited tools on this empty ranch?

My father and I tried to walk as nonchalantly as possible back to the house so the moms wouldn't get worried. We opened the old cabin closet and rooted out a pitchfork and shovel. Suspicions rose as we turned to leave with those items tucked beneath our arms. A quick answer that "Everything's fine" was all my mother got as we raced back to the river.

The boys had held a solid line of defense with rocks in hand as the other dad kept an eye on the snake's whereabouts. It was up on the bank next to the trail. I fell in line at the back with my own rock poised in the air.

A lightning-fast stab with the pitchfork held the snake in place as the shovel was brought down behind its head. It took a couple chops, but soon the head was relieved of its body that squirmed aimlessly.

Our triumphant hollers and clapping brought the moms outside where they expressed how they were "glad that no one had gotten hurt."

As we walked back to the cabin, I felt as if I had become a brave survivalist like the boy in *Hatchet*. It was not the first time I had seen my father kill a snake that threatened us, nor would it be the last. We didn't live in the country, but it seemed to occur rather regularly that we would be on some father/daughter camp out or family camping trip and he would spring into action. When threatened he is an *act first, think later* kind of guy, and I once witnessed his swift decapitation of a snake using a plastic frisbee. Thankfully, he has quick reflexes and was an athlete, so he never got hurt. However, I should note that Dad never recommended that any of his kids utilize these same methods.

Nonetheless, I still find myself carrying a frisbee in my car... just in case.

FALL
Winter
Aa Bb Cc Dd Ee Ff Gg Hh Ii Jj Kk
Welcome

3

New School, New Look

I was walking into my first day of fourth grade in a brand new school. I should have been excited. I should have been proudly showing off my new outfit, or at the very least, chatting with the one friend I knew would be in my class…instead I was hiding behind a stack of books, hoping I was invisible.

Then it happened. As I found my seat in our homeroom, a boy caught a glimpse of my face and his eyes widened. He tried to look away, but he just couldn't. The fact is: once one guy starts staring it's hard for others not to as well. So before the bell had even rung I could hear the whispers.

In the poor kid's defense, I don't know that I could have kept from staring if I had seen my face that day in class either. I wasn't mad, just embarrassed. And itchy.

Finally one brave soul asked what had happened to me and I was able to explain that I didn't always look like a red, bloated, blotchy alien—I just was recovering from an allergic reaction to poison ivy.

The sigh of relief was almost palpable.

Within a few days I had made good friends, and started liking my new school. But I never forgot what it felt like to be the new kid. Or to look for a leaf of three and let it be!

HOLY BIBLE

4

Doesn’t Look Like It Tastes

As a pastor’s kid, I had taken “communion” dozens of times. Our church always used Welch’s grape juice, just like we drank at home. I always had been a fan of any bread product and was happy to partake no matter how stale the cracker.

One summer we were on a mission trip visiting some Italian missionaries. These people had started an Italian-language church, an internet cafe, and an international church. They could also add to their achievements “Changed communion for Jessica forever.”

On Sunday we were in service, singing in English and listening to a sermon in Italian and English when the music stopped and my dad nudged me. He warned me that we were about to take communion. I smiled and nodded, having heard the same thing. The trays came and we took the bread without incident. Soon after, Dad passed me a small cup. Looking at me warily, he took a sip of his. I was thirsty so I decided to gulp my grape juice down.

A burning realization hit immediately. This was not in fact grape juice. It was wine! I coughed and spluttered, making quite the scene. We were on the front row as the guests of honor, and I saw the pastor smile as he acknowledged my distress. My brothers fared no better, and I think one even left to find a bathroom.

The worst part wasn't the stares from other congregants or parents. It was that awful aftertaste and dryness in my mouth. I practically leaped out of my chair after the closing prayer to find a water fountain.

I learned that day a practice I religiously follow in every setting: take a quick sniff to make sure you know what you are drinking before you choke in front of everyone.

On another trip, my family took a cruise ship to get among some Greek islands where Dad was teaching. My brothers and I loved the kid area, the views from the deck, and the endless stream of food. It was impossible to go hungry there.

Some of the food did look kind of weird, but we would just avoid those dishes and swap them out for something safe and reliable like mac and cheese or burgers.

One day we had been playing and chasing one another around the deck and worked up quite the appetite, so I wasn't thinking as cautiously as we entered the dining room. I saw the big people enjoying a plate of what I assumed to be onion rings, and I dove in. I was considering the especially chewy texture and thinking that European onions must be different from American ones, when my dad piped up, "Wow. I am so proud of you for trying octopus. How do you like it?"

I reflexively opened my mouth and dumped its contents into my napkin before running to the bathroom.

In this case I learned an important rule: if the adults are enjoying it and you can't recognize it, don't eat it.

5

The Cat Goes for a Ride

I will start by pleading childish stupidity and stating that I do not condone animal cruelty of any kind. I grew up with dogs who were more than willing to play. On several occasions, I dressed our poor dachshund up in doll clothes or pushed her around in my baby carriage and saw no extreme adverse side effects.

The kitten seemed friendly and curious. She was patting at a string of yarn on my friend's bed when the idea hit me. Wouldn't it be awesome if we could take the cat for a ride? She was the perfect size to fit in my friend's Barbie car.

Without another thought, I grabbed the kitten and stuffed her into the small vehicle. My friend fetched a piece of cardboard to keep the kitten from escaping the convertible, and off we went.

Zooming the car down the hallway, we could begin to hear frantic meows and clawing. By the time we got around the corner to the living room, the cardboard was beginning to disintegrate as the cat tried to claw her way to freedom.

When we looked up into the horrified face of my friend's mom, we knew we had made a grave error. As we removed the cardboard, per her mother's command, a streak of grey fur and claws flew out of the car and zipped down the hall.

While being reprimanded for our lack in judgement and abuse of toys and the kitten, I could feel the sting of the claw marks on my hand. The scratches were surface wounds and (here I quote my buddy's mother) "nothing compared to the emotional trauma" we had just put the beloved cat through.

After being bandaged, we went in search of the cat to make amends. We searched everywhere and couldn't find the kitty. Finally, on our fifth patrol through the house, we heard a terrifying hissing coming from her parent's bedroom. I turned into the room and was struck by glowing eyes full of hatred, glaring out from the farthest reaches underneath the bed. I was about to bend down and pet the animal when my friend wisely cautioned that I had done enough "playing" with the cat for one day.

I later found out that the poor thing hid under that bed for several days before it would venture out again. Further, my friend's Barbie car was covered in scratches from the inside—a continued reminder that cats do not like car rides.

Now I just give them soft pets.

6

Using My Head

It was sunny. The sun was in my eyes. At least, that is what I would tell people afterward.

They say that with practice comes perfection. I believe I disprove this saying. I had practiced. I had practiced in drills with my team, with my parents, and even on my own. In our backyard I would practice catching pop fly balls by throwing the softball up on the roof and catching it with my glove before it hit the ground. It could get tricky when you threw the ball up at an angle and it came rolling back opposite from where you were. So, I figured I was getting some good practice.

Then came game day. Practice was over. It was time to test my skills.

We all heard the bang of the aluminum bat as the hitter lobbed it up into the sky. I was in the outfield and perfectly positioned to make any easy out.

I called out to my teammates that "I got it!" But as I backed up with my glove held high, I lost sight of the ball.

Suddenly—wham! My head was throbbing and I was on the ground.

Within moments, my whole team was running to me to make sure that I was OK. Unfortunately, the runner was not concerned with my well-being, and she kept running.

All I could hear was a deafening roar of shouts of parents (my father the loudest) to "Go get the ball! She's headed for third!"

Thankfully, someone tossed it to our catcher and she chased the runner back to third base before the "easy out" turned into a home run. However, she and two other players from their team crossed home plate in that inning, securing our fate.

As I got older, I found that the softball no longer only attacked me in the outfield. The danger followed me to home plate. Being rather small, I almost always took my base via a walk. I was able to scrunch my small body so that my strike zone virtually disappeared. Our coaches loved it. The other pitchers did not.

As their frustration grew over a few seasons, my on-base percentage stayed very high; however, instead of walking, I was hobbling down to first after being hit by pitches. Over and over again I went to first base with bruises on my arms, legs, and face. Finally, after a second black eye, I decided that maybe there was a safer way to spend my weekends.

Sometimes your will or desire to do something well just isn't enough if you lack the God-given talent. So, I shifted to something I knew I would be good at—theatre! More on that later...

7

Almost Buried Alive

In my hurry to get back to the cabin after breakfast, I almost squashed him. He was right there in the middle of the road! I scooped up the sluggish toad and took him back to my cabin. I couldn't stand the thought of just leaving him out there to get run over.

Setting him in a cup with water and some sticks, I left with my group to go on a day hike. It was a beautiful day, warm while slightly overcast. Everyone enjoyed the walk so much that we were out a little longer than planned. By the time we got back, I was concerned about the state of my poor toad.

His dazed state had given way to paralysis. We couldn't even find a pulse. Heartbroken, I tried to revive my friend with small compressions on his chest—but alas, he was a goner. Our counselor was not pleased to have a toad as a house guest, much less a dead one, so I took him out behind the cabin to give him a respectable burial.

I dug the hole with my bare hands as it started to drizzle rain. A tear escaped the corner of my eye, mixing with the rain. I spoke a prayer over the toad, bidding him goodbye. But when

I reached over to grab the body, I found nothing! He was gone! Confused as to how he could have rolled away, I scanned the area and spotted a toad hopping furiously toward some underbrush.

I had to go back inside and admit, to my horror, that I had almost buried my four-legged buddy while he was still alive. As embarrassing as it was to admit this, I was happy to see him go back into his home. Next time you see a toad in the road just remember to leave him be. I know one who wishes that I had!

SCIENCE

8

Rejection: Cute Boys and Seating Assignments

His hair was perfect—or perfect for 2001—his smile was sparkling white and he had a carefree *laissez-faire* attitude that relaxed me. I had been lucky enough to sit next to him for the first three seat rotations and my sixth-grade heart was pounding as the final seat assignment was given for the year.

I had a big smile on my face and was holding my breath in anticipation—hoping my crush and I would be able to work together for one more rotation before our elementary experience ended and middle school began. As the teacher picked up her carefully crafted list, he turned toward me and our eyes met.

I waited with baited breath to hear him say something like, "I hope we get to stay together." Instead he crushed me with one short whispered sentence. "No offence," he said, "but, I really hope we get different partners this time."

I think my cheeks went fifty shades of red as I mumbled some agreement back to him and stared at my desk, wishing it would swallow me up. I wanted to say, "If you have to preface something with 'no offense' then you probably shouldn't say it!"

Crushed, I moved with the flock of other students as we settled into our new seating arrangements. I would like to say that I learned something, but I think all I walked away with that day was that sixth grade boys were dumb and insensitive.

9

Middle School: The Nemesis of Rain Puddles

The rain was pounding down upon the pavement and making a small lake in front of the cafeteria doors. Once again, I was starting at a new school. But this year I would be sporting glasses, braces, and expanders. I knew I was never going to win any popularity contests, but I had been hoping to not be soaking wet walking into my seventh-grade year.

I shouldered my backpack and jumped out of the van, sprinting for those big glass doors. I had been pretty quick and my backpack had made a fairly decent umbrella, so I wasn't as wet as I thought I'd be. I actually felt pretty good, like I had passed the first test of middle school.

Excited to see a friendly face, my best friend, smiling and waving me over to meet her friends, I began to run as I crossed the threshold. That was when it happened. That was the moment gravity betrayed me and I flew backwards to a chorus of laughter.

I had slipped on a massive puddle just inside, flinging my glasses and books in every direction. The laughter continued as I attempted to recover my belongings and quietly slink away towards my friend at a back table. I was sure I had blown it, that I would never live down that cartoonish sprawl upon the cafeteria floor.

Here is the good news—after almost crying at dinner as I told my parents about my less-than-stellar beginning to my middle school career, they began laughing. After the shock wore off, I was able to laugh as well, picturing what I must have looked like.

Within a few days everyone had forgotten about it and I ended up having the best year ever.

10

High School: Directionally and Vertically Challenged

I am short. You can call me fun size, or vertically challenged, but the fact was that once I got to high school I was still the same size as I was in sixth grade praying for a late growth spurt.

I had toured the school with my mom once I had received my schedule before school began. Everyone who knows me also knows that I am severely directionally challenged. I once got lost a block from my house walking home from the park. So, the hope was that I would be able to memorize the route and get to where I needed to go, even with a limited line of sight.

The first day of ninth grade finally came. I got to all my classes on time. Things were going well, when the lunch bell rang, and I panicked.

I walked to my locker on the other side of the school, reciting my locker combination in my head while being pushed ahead by the masses. Once I got there I had some trouble getting the combination right as I was standing on my tiptoes to reach it. By the time I finally had gotten my lunch and books for my afternoon classes, the halls had emptied. I no longer had a crowd to push me toward the cafeteria. I had taken too long.

Suddenly in a panic, I ran toward the nearest staircase and tried to go down. But a hall monitor was just around the corner and I was terrified I would get in trouble for not being where I was supposed to be. So I went to the other side of the building to attempt an escape at a smaller staircase there, but alas another teacher was stationed nearby. I glanced at the clock and saw in horror I only had fifteen minutes left to eat before my next class... so I went to the bathroom.

I sat in a stall eating my lunch, embarrassed, trying not to cry. This was my first day of high school and here I was hiding in a gross bathroom stall.

I wish that I could say that was the only embarrassing moment of my high school career. But that would be lying. I eventually learned to just ask for help and not be afraid of teachers. But the embarrassing moments would unfortunately continue.

It was still my freshman year when some months later I was going up the large grand staircase at the front of our school to get to my math tutorials before school. Suddenly I felt a rush of wind, BO, and clattering shoes fly down the steps past me as the football team did some training inside on this particularly rainy day. I caught a glance of a cute guy and was turning my head to nod "hello" when gravity yet again attacked. I fell up the stairs as the players zoomed past, trying to not step on me or my binders.

Falling down stairs is one thing, but I had fallen *up* the stairs in front of the entire football team. If my first day had not humbled me, this certainly did. High school was really good at that—college was even better at it. Needless to say, none of those guys ever asked me out.

PARLOR
SET

11

Shaky Sets

My heart was pounding. I had somehow landed the lead role as a freshman. The posted cast listing declared that I was to portray one of the charming (if also misguided and deadly) elderly sisters in *Arsenic and Old Lace*. We were astonished that I got the lead! In fact, my mom had actually brought Kleenex in the car as we drove to the high school to see the cast list, ready for disappointing news.

I threw myself into the role: working hard to memorize all my lines, bonding with the cast to develop great timing, perfecting my old lady voice and walk. We rehearsed every scene for what felt like a thousand times. Unfortunately, we had not rehearsed with the stage set fully completed. There had been no time before opening night.

All went fine, until the start of the second act. I became trapped behind a door, unable to enter center stage. The door was stuck. The uncomfortable pause of fellow actors waiting for my entrance seemed to drag on forever. Someone started covering with ad lib while I slammed myself against the door full force. I finally broke in—literally—several lines late.

As the other actors and a packed house stared at me, I rubbed my shoulder and said, "I need to get that door fixed." It was all I could come up with in the moment. Sadly, this was not the only incident we had with this set. On another night, the actor who portrayed my brother was marching around the stage playing the bugle when his foot broke through the stairs. His leg hung there stuck for a minute as he stiffened with shock. He recovered fairly quickly and proceeded to hurry down the rest of the steps before any others could give way.

Another time we were rehearsing our play for the state One Act competition. We were caught up in the flow of a smooth scene when I realized that the actress next to me was taking a long time to sip her fake iced drink and get out her line. In fact, she was starting to look panicked. She touched at her throat and then leaned against a piece of furniture. Holy smokes, the girl was choking! Before I could get behind her to perform the Heimlich (at which I felt less than confident), a fake ice cube flew out of her mouth. The deep breath she took was immediately joined by all of ours.

Many years later, I was a judge for a speech and debate competition at my alma mater. I was heartbroken when a young man came in, began his speech, and then stopped. I asked him if he was alright, and he told me he had forgotten his speech. I told him that I could pretend he didn't say that, and he could just keep going. But he had a meltdown and left the room. He wouldn't even try to go on.

There are more stories I could tell: of the time our crew backstage ate the apples that I was supposed to peel in a later scene; of having to use a window as an exit when another door didn't open; or of my yarn rolling into the orchestra pit as the curtain rose on the first scene. But surely you already grasp my point. In any play there will be things that go wrong. Sets break, entrances are missed, and props disappear. The crew and actors who shine are those that keep going. The audience doesn't know you made a mistake unless you tell them. In real life we also must be able to "go with the flow," to make adjustments as circumstances change or calls don't go our way. If a performer just stands there staring into those blinding lights, sweating, then he or she can't move on with the scene. In the same way, you can't move on with your life if you refuse to make the adjustments needed to move forward. Don't be afraid. Don't quit. Just keep going.

12

Crosswalks and Close Calls

I didn't even want to be there. Unlike almost everyone else in the room, I felt no imperative need for me to get my driver's license. I was happy to be driven around by friends and family. Driving school was quite unpleasant. The warning videos were terrifying, it seemed strange to take driver's education in a shopping mall, and the loud three-pack-a-day voice of the chief instructor made me want to clear my throat.

After memorizing a bunch of rules I doubted that I would remember, we finally got to start our driving sessions with instructors. I was matched with a kind, quiet Hispanic man for my driving instructor. He spoke little English but used what command he had to make us hypervigilant at all times. He stuck a banana in the tailpipe once, just to make sure that we looked over the vehicle before starting it. He would crank up the Disney station so that I could barely hear his soft-spoken turning directions. After all his training, one would think I was prepared for the day the chief instructor had me drive with her. But one would be mistaken.

I was near panic. I hated driving on the highway. Just getting out of the roundabout road around the mall—or "circle of death" as I liked to call it—was challenging enough. I managed to clear the circle of death and followed the chief teacher's instructions to enter the highway. Somehow, we survived, and I was next directed into a neighborhood. All this was achieved while being constantly harassed by the instructor. Unlike my banana-loving teacher, the boss was not quiet. She spoke English fluently and quite loudly. I was faced with a constant barrage of questions like: "Did you check that mirror first?"

"Why did you stop before the line?"

"Why did you leave your indicator on so long?"

By the time we were pulling into the parking lot at the end of our session I was rattled. I looked at the instructor to see if there was anything I had missed on the last turn through the circle of death. Unfortunately, this meant that I did not see the older lady...walking through the crosswalk in front of me...pushing a baby stroller. The instructor screamed, I hit the brakes hard, and we stopped inches from her. The lady just smiled at me and puttered on.

After signing out, I saw the woman in the mall and walked up to apologize to her for the close call. She laughed, smiled, and said, "Oh honey, that's alright. That was the most excitement I have had in weeks!" I was tempted to ask her to go relay that message to the instructor, whom I imagined writing out my arrest warrant.

Against all odds, I did get my driver's license that year. For a time, I continued to look for a banana in my tailpipe before I started my car.

13

Summer Nanny: Dead Bunnies and the Discovery Channel

The blood-curdling screams startled all of us. They sounded almost like a human baby, but high and cut short. The cries of the young daughter once she reached the backyard may have come close to matching them though.

The family I was nannying for had a big dog. He was a sweetie. But unfortunately today as I entered the backyard I saw that he had chosen to play with a most unlucky rabbit. There was blood dripping from his mouth and a half-dead bunny clenched between his jaws. The little girl and her brother were crying and screaming at the dog to drop it. He was instead proud of his catch and was trying to show it off to them.

When the boy grabbed a stick to hit the dog and make him drop it, I finally snapped out of my state of shock and ran to get the stick away. Too late, the dog had been punished and dropped his prize before he could finish extinguishing its life and put it out of its misery. A shoe box was found and the rabbit placed inside as the children hoped for a miraculous recovery and I got the dog put away.

Not surprisingly, the rescue attempt failed and the real crying began. The little girl was beside herself. So I had her go inside while I "took care" of the bunny.

I walked in to find her watching a cute puppy on one of those animal rescue shows. I thought this would be cathartic—see an animal being saved and living happily ever after...

...boy was I wrong.

In a flash of an instant, the puppy's life was hanging in the balance and things were heading south fast. Before I could find the controller to change the channel, they were covering the dead patient with a sheet.

Within the hour I was on the phone trying to explain to the mother why her daughter had locked herself in her room crying hysterically and the son was now drawing pictures of a dog dripping with blood. She came home to make sure the bunny was disposed of and calm the storm of hormones emitting from the young preteen's room.

That day I learned a valuable lesson: never turn on the Discovery Channel with kids around.

14

Pooping Directions

There was a smile on his face that I knew meant trouble. His pants were still around his ankles when he waddled out of the bathroom. I looked at the other leader in the room and saw that she was holding one screaming kid while another was grabbing for some snacks on the counter. So, I walked over and stooped down.

I pulled up his pants and asked him, "Did you wash your hands?"

"No," he replied with his lilting two-year-old voice.

"Well, we need to do that," I answered as I took his hand and we walked back into the bathroom.

It smelled bad, but I ignored it and helped him up onto the stool to wash his hands. I gave directions: "Use the soap"…"scrub scrub scrub your hands"…"OK, now dry them"…"On the paper towel, not your shirt!" Like most kids his age, he needed constant encouragement and guidance on how to complete this task.

As I turned to leave the restroom, I saw it. Against the wall. A pile of poop.

"What is that?" I asked the boy.

"My poop!" he declared with a proud smile shining on his face.

"What do you mean? Why would you do that? We poop in the toilet! I asked you before you came in here if you knew how to use the potty..." I stopped. Suddenly it hit me...I never directly told him to poop in the potty. I merely directed him to go to the bathroom.

Thus, I learned that when sending a toddler to the bathroom you have to give very clear directions. Otherwise, when they come out you had better be ready with Clorox wipes—a lot of them.

CAMP

15

Prayer Requests: Santa vs. Jesus

We were on the verge of World War Three. The pitches of their third-grade girl voices were getting higher, tear ducts were starting to fill, and once they stood up I knew I had to intervene.

It wasn't a brawl in the school lunchroom nor was it a fight at a friend's house over a boy.

This was the result of asking for prayer requests.

I was a camp counselor for third-grade girls and it was only half-way through the summer.

The argument did not begin with any deep theological queries about the universe, but by a request for a girl's dead cat's soul.

Yup, a dead cat started it all.

We were sitting on comfy couches, had just completed a rather inspiring conversation about obeying authority, and it had gotten late so I was starting to drift.

"Please pray that Booty's soul is in heaven and that she is OK..."

Before I could give some sort of comforting word and move to the next girl in the circle, a girl (with a streak of honesty that almost rivaled my own) piped up with: "That's stupid—animals don't go to heaven. They just die and then rot in the ground. Everyone knows that."

As my mind tried to file through all of the comforting, while not super offensive and biblically-sound responses I could give (which there really weren't many to choose from), another voice jumped on an even more dangerous rabbit trail.

"Do you think Jesus or Santa has more magic?"

Our lover of truth immediately answered this question to fill the void with, "There is no Santa Claus!"

"Yes there is!!!!"

Suddenly our sweet, good-natured prayer circle had drawn a line in the sand and it was Santa vs. Jesus.

My co-counselor stared at me in horror as tempers and voices rose. She was a deer in headlights, and I was the hunter searching for any quick solution.

"Jesus isn't magic, Santa Claus is. Close your eyes, bow your heads, 'cause I'm gonna pray!"

I made it a nice long prayer to give a chance for tempers to quiet down.

By the time I had finished reading chapter three of *The Lion, the Witch and the Wardrobe* all was smiles and snores.

World War Three had been averted; and a couple college counselors learned the dangers of prayer request circles.

16

The RA Adventures

When we had our resident advisor training before the year began, we talked about what to do if one of our freshmen was exhibiting signs of depression, how the toilet paper was to be distributed, and how to check guys in and out of the dorm on open visiting nights (I went to a Baptist college). I understood that I would be taking on a special role in these young lives as we helped them navigate their first year of college with offers to talk, events for them at which they could get to know others, and an open door policy whenever anyone was in need.

Never once did we discuss what to do if there was a threatening message found in glow in the dark paint on a student's wall. I honestly don't know if it would have helped if we *had* discussed it.

My roommate and I were falling asleep after a late night study session when the air suddenly exploded with screams, slamming doors, and pounding feet. I opened our door to see a herd of terrified young women clawing to get into our room. After we had calmed down a bit, I went to their room to see what had scared them so much. Low and behold, sure enough, there was a message of a threatening nature glowing in green on their wall.

In the end—after a police report was filed—and an investigation conducted, it was found to be a macabre joke between the ladies from the previous year over a horror movie they had watched. Unfortunately they had forgotten about it and not scrubbed it away at the end of the year, thus scaring the living daylights (or nighlights) out of two freshmen.

Later that same year I received a call from our dorm "mom" saying that there was a shopping cart in front of the dorm that needed to go—now! It was a visiting weekend for parents coming up and stolen merch was not the first image they wanted in the view of parents as they pulled up to the dorm.

It did not take long for me to find the responsible party. Apparently they had "borrowed" the shopping cart to take some cute pics for their Facebook page with it, but were now too scared to return it. They had been informed that what they committed was theft and looked up the fine. They were convinced that they would be caught on camera returning it and would lose scholarships, and ultimately, have their lives ruined.

I tried to assure them that they were making a mountain out of a molehill and they were probably not going to get in trouble. Bottom line: the cart had to be gone within 24 hours.

After much deliberation, the young ladies drove an hour away to the next town's Walmart to return the cart. I doubt that our Walmart ever missed it, but if they did, that's where it is.

There are numerous other entertaining accounts I could give you about my adventures as an RA involving a massive spider that met his end via stiletto at 2 a.m., an exorcism attempt, and a social club project disaster that involved way too much glitter. But I will spare you. Suffice it to say I was never bored!

17

As the Intern: Tornados, Lock-in Disasters, and Chasing a Tortoise

I graduated college with big aspirations of changing the world, but I didn't know how or where. So I went to a church in Oklahoma to intern for the summer and waited for the large flashing sign I was sure God would send my way showing me what to do next.

That summer began with me spending my first night in the grandparent's storm shelter during a tornado as my grandmother worried if she had left the stove on. It was dark and cramped with my grandparents, myself, their three dogs, and a neighbor with her pooch. We gratefully emerged some time later to find the house perfectly fine and intact (with the stove off). Unfortunately, many others in the area did not fare as well, and I got to start work a week early sorting donations for the tornado victims. It was neat to see so many people giving all they could for others in their community. This was a rough wake-up call to start my internship.

I was asked later to plan and lead a lock-in for the youth. I had loved these growing up—doing fun activities, eating junk food, hanging with friends, and using all of your willpower not to fall asleep while hanging out at the church all night. So I heartily agreed and took on the challenge to create a night these youth would never forget. I was successful in making it memorable, but not for the reasons I had imagined.

Everything started out smoothly with some worship music and a lesson that they seemed to really get into. We then went outside to play a fun game I had found on the internet. That is when things began to take a turn.

The students stood on either side of a volleyball net with a blanket stretched between them and began flinging a raw chicken over the net. The goal being to not let it touch the ground (online the turkey had been cooked). Suddenly there were screams as bits of raw chicken flew through the air and into a student's face. Some of the guys kept the game going until there was not much left on the blanket and chicken covered the field.

Before the end of the night this motley crew broke a clock on the wall, got a student stuck in the dryer, and played a game of hide-and-seek that ended with a couple being found sleeping in a closet.

Good intentions but really poor planning. I was relieved to hear the youth ministry was only on the hook for something like sixty bucks for the clock. Best of all—when the parents came they each found a child to take home with them.

I was relieved when it came time for Vacation Bible School that summer and all I had to do was the Bible story skit and watch over a few stations the kids went through. On the second-to-last day of the week-long adventure, a volunteer brought in some animals for the kids to look at. I had gathered each group outside, sitting with hands in their laps ready to watch and listen. One boy was having a particularly hard time sitting still, but managed to stay seated until the presentation was over. The turtle that he had been eyeing had wandered a little ways away, and he had been itching to pet it. So I said he could.

Before I knew it, the little boy had jumped up, began running, and fallen onto the concrete. As I swooped in before any moms could see the damage, I had to push down a gag reflex at the blood pouring from his mouth.

He didn't end up needing any stitches and he enjoyed the popsicle on his busted lip. However, having to explain to his mom that he had been injured chasing a turtle did make me laugh. Thankfully, the mom laughed too.

18

Handling the Snake: Why King Tut got Angry

As the program kicked off with kids' laughter, I thought I heard an odd hissing noise and looked around.

To my surprise, it was coming from the empty trash can I had been instructed to open.

With some hesitation, I lifted the lid and stifled a screech.

I had only been working as an intern at the camp for a week at this point.

I hadn't come to a full understanding of their hands-on approach to outdoor education, so when I was told to stand backstage and grab the "snake" from the bucket with the lid on it, I had assumed it would be fake.

Instead, I had the very angry eyes of a long, very alive snake staring at me.

There was an arm-length metal claw I was to use to pick up King Tut, but as I reached in, he coiled and struck the rod. A shriek escaped my lips and the trash can toppled over as I pulled my arm back.

The angry King Tut was now on the loose in a closet—with me.

Quickly, I grabbed the trash can with one hand and used the claw to shove him out from under the table he had retreated beneath. Immediately, I threw the trash can over him.

I now had a trapped angry snake that needed to be ready for the stage in one minute. The cue for me to hand off the snake came and I knew I had to grab him. So as the door to the stage flew open and my coworker thrust his hand into the closet for a snake, I flipped the bucket with clenched teeth, picked him up near the head with the claw and at the tail in my hand, and threw him toward the door in one fluid motion.

Thankfully, my coworker was ready and caught him. Even with all of the commotion he could see my face was white as a sheet. "Are you OK?"

"Oh yeah, I'm good."

Getting King Tut back into the bucket so he could be taken back to his cage was a picnic, comparatively. He was still upset, but the kids had worn him out. In the end, the kids learned about snakes, and I learned that King Tut had an attitude.

CAMP

19

Hunt, Cook, Eat: A Stream, a Rock and a Squirrel

Hunt, cook, eat. The exercise is as simple as it sounds. You give the kids a map, GPS, and compass to find their dinner hidden on the property after which they cook it and then eat it. It is supposed to be deceptively simple with few instructions, allowing for creativity, collaboration, and teamwork. Some groups were really fast at catching on and we were back in our cabins by nine p.m.—others took a little longer.

I was still working at the camp as an intern and loving it. As I looked at my group that day, I noticed the girl with the map was not speaking up and we were headed for a big creek. As we approached it, I stated that I was not going to get wet crossing it—hoping this would make the kid with the map speak up and point out the bridge nearby. Instead, a burly high school boy said "What if I carry you? Can we cross then?"

Before I could think of how to phrase my reply, he had picked me up and carried me across the stream as his class soaked their shoes following us.

By the three-hour mark they were yelling and fighting and saying that so-and-so had led them wrong, he didn't know how to work a GPS, etc., I was standing back watching and waiting for the magical moment when a group would come together, put aside quarrels, and each take a responsibility. Instead, one vocal young man looked at me with an unpleasant gleam in his eye and stated, "I am starving; we could always resort to eating her if we have to and say that she got lost." Thankfully, the teacher with this school group jumped in to remind him of the illegal and messy nature of cannibalism.

As the teacher was speaking though, I saw the ravenous look in the student's eyes turn to a squirrel clambering up a tree a few feet away. He grabbed a rock and threw with scary accuracy at the poor creature. All of the kids screamed, either from horror or from teenage all-consuming hunger, and began to run.

Thankfully, the teacher and I were able to subdue the squirrel boy before any fatalities occurred (he had missed his mark by an inch), pep talked to the group, and ended up eating the yummy meal that was waiting for them.

In the end, I found that the hunger of a teenage boy can be a powerful and dangerous force—and always carried some granola bars with me after that.

20

Fish Funerals

I tried to warn her that I had a bad history with fish. I had begun killing off pet fish at a young age by trying to feed them my Oreos, or giving them heart attacks when changing their water without checking the temperature. I had one fish die and I never even noticed until I cleaned the tank a month later and found his remains under a rock that he had been trapped beneath. Finally, when I had a fish actually commit suicide—jumping out of the bowl while the tank was being cleaned and flopping under furniture—I decided to call it quits. I could almost hear the cheers of fish everywhere.

I had given a lot of toilet bowl funerals to my fish and had no desire to perform another. But my roommate convinced me to take on the role of fish caregiver one more time as she explained that it was only going to be for a couple of days and all I had to do was feed them.

I fed the fish when I got up the next morning and again when I got home. I even remembered to turn on their light for a little bit. I went to sleep thinking that maybe now as a college graduate

I was finally mature and capable enough to care for a living creature. Then the alarm went off and I went to feed them...

I counted, then recounted, and sure enough there were two missing. How? How could I possibly have lost two fish? While sleeping? As I surveyed the scene in my panicked state, I noticed a fin stuck in the filter. Apparently one guy had made a failed escape attempt via the filter, and I had to clean out his remains. Then I noticed one rather fat fish, it looked bloated or pregnant—and suddenly the horrible thought came to me—this fish had eaten his brother! I swear I fed them breakfast and dinner the day before, yet somehow on my watch they decide to have a mutiny.

I didn't call my roommate but instead waited until she got back the next day to tell her in person about the fates of her pets. I felt terrible. I explained the situation, best as I could figure, and waited for her to lose it. Instead she looked at the tank, back at me, and said, "Wow. You really are bad with fish."

I have not since cared for another fish, only dogs for friends and family, and I can happily report that all have survived—thus far. My husband and I are getting a dog this summer; pray for her.

Conclusion: It's Going to be OK

I hope I made you laugh. That I made you think. Maybe you paused and saw that your huge mistakes and rejections are just a small piece of your story. These pieces never look pretty on their own, but pieced together, they create a beautiful picture.

Being a kid is tough, a preteen is even tougher, and a teen at times is unbearably hard. There are a million voices all telling you what to do, how to get better, that you are not enough, that the bad grade you got or a relationship that broke will haunt you forever. These come from the media, leaders, friends, family, and even yourself. Some of these people are genuinely trying to help, and others are just trying to hurt you. Everything you do or say seems permanently tattooed into history with each Tweet, Snapchat, InstaPic, and YouTube video. It can make you feel like you are trapped. But you are not. You are free. Free to choose what you will do next. Pick yourself up after your mistakes and embarrassing moments, learn from them, then brush them off and keep going forward. Yucky stuff happens, don't let it define you.

Remember this: You are of value. You have worth. The world needs to hear what you have to say. Don't give up on your dreams. Keep moving forward. And if your feet should ever bring you by my doorstep, I would love to travel with you. We can trip and fall to the finish line together!

About the Author

Jessica Anders is a teacher in the Frisco Independent School District in Texas. She teaches special-needs middle schooler students and has previous experience in camping and youth ministry. She lives in Little Elm, Texas, with her husband Grant—who loves to laugh at (we mean with) her adventures—and their dog, Penelope.

About the Illustrator

Tim Hodge is an animator, storyboard artist, animation director, illustrator and author. He has been in the animation industry for over 25 years working on projects including Disney's, *The Lion King*, *Mulan*, and *Brother Bear* as well as Big Idea Productions' *Veggie Tales* films, *Lyle the Kindly Viking*, and *The Ballad of Little Joe* which he directed. Tim was the Executive Producer of the *3-2-1 Penguins!* series on NBC and the program *VeggieTales in the House*, on which he collaborated, (Dreamworks/Netflix) and was nominated for a Daytime Emmy award. He has created for DreamworksTV, Warner Brothers TV Animation and his newest book, *Pith and Vinegar* is available now.